EYES ON NATURE®

MIGHTY DINOSAURS

Kidsbooks®

Table of Contents

Written by
Rebecca L. Grambo

Scientific Consultants

Mark A. Norell
Chair of the Division of Paleontology
American Museum of Natural History

Carl Mehling
Scientific Assistant of Herpetology
Amercan Museum of Nature History

Fossils

How do we know so much about organisms that are not around any more? The answers lie in fossils.

Fossils are evidence of ancient living things. By studying them, paleontologists (*see glossary*) can learn about dinosaurs and other life from long ago.

Fossils are not just bones. Many things can be fossilized, including teeth, wood, shells, and footprints, or faint impressions of skin, feathers, or leaves.

How does something become a fossil? Usually, it happens like this:

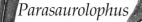

Parasaurolophus

Becoming a Fossil

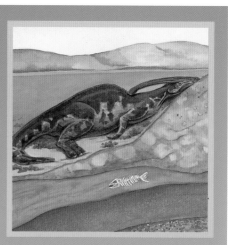

The dead organism sinks to the bottom of a lake, river, or sea. Some of its body rots or is eaten.

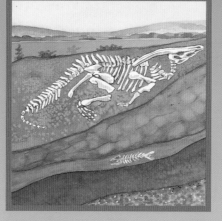

Whatever is left of the organism (usually, the hard parts, like bones) becomes covered with fine mud.

A lot of time passes. Gradually, the original remains are replaced with minerals and becomes part of the surrounding rock.

More time passes. The water dries up, or rocks are pushed to the surface. Wind and weather wear down the rock until the fossil is close enough to the surface to be found.

4

They Weren't All Dinosaurs

Rhamphorhynchus, a pterosaur of dinosaur times, was not a dinosaur.

Mastodonsaurus, one of the largest amphibians that ever lived, lived in dinosaur times but was not a dinosaur.

Non-avian dinosaurs were reptiles that lived on Earth in prehistoric times. Most of them died out about 65 million years ago, but they inhabited Earth for more than 160 million years before that! Hundreds of species of dinosaur lived during the Mesozoic Period (not all at the same time). Not every now-extinct reptile that lived at that time was a dinosaur. Pterosaurs, such as the *Rhamphorhynchus* above, were not dinosaurs. Neither were many reptiles that swam in lakes or seas. Most non-avian dinosaurs were land animals, but nondinosaur reptiles lived on land, too.

Elasmosaurus, a large sea reptile that lived in dinosaur times, was not a dinosaur.

DID YOU KNOW. . . ?
The word *dinosaur* means "fearfully great lizard."

Dinosaur Types

Dinosaurs are divided into two main groups, based on their hip bones. Saurischian (saw-RISH-ee-un) dinosaurs have hips that look sort of like a lizard's. Ornithischian (or-nuh-THISH-ee-un) dinosaurs have hips that look more like a bird's, but it was the saurischian dinosaurs that gave rise to birds.

SAURISCHIANS
(LIZARD-HIPPED DINOSAURS)
There are two main types of saurischians.

Left to right: *Ceratosaurus, Ornithomimus, Tyrannosaurus, Coelophysis, Allosaurus,* and *Deinonychus.*

THEROPODS
(The name means "beast-footed.")
• most long-extinct ones ate meat; some may have eaten meat and fruit
• most had sharp teeth and claws (though some were toothless)
• most walked on strong back legs; were swift runners
• birds are today's theropods

SAUROPODS
(The name means "lizard-footed.")
• ate plants
• had a heavy body, a long neck and tail, and tall, tree-like legs
• walked on four legs

Left to right: *Cetiosaurus, Camarasaurus, Opisthocoelicaudia, Brachiosaurus, Mamenchisaurus,* and *Diplodocus.*

ORNITHISCHIANS
(BIRD-HIPPED DINOSAURS)
There are three main types of ornithischians.

ORNITHOPODS
(The name means "bird-footed"—though few had feet that look like a bird's.)
- ate plants
- probably stood on their back legs as well as all four
- had beaklike mouths
- had three or four clawed toes

From left to right: *Ouranosaurus, Iguanodon, Heterodontosaurus, Parasaurolophus*, and *Hypsilophodon*.

From left to right: *Psittacosaurus, Triceratops, Styracosaurus, Torosaurus, Pentaceratops,* and *Protoceratops*.

MARGINOCEPHALIANS
(The name means "margin heads.")
- ate plants
- most had horns on their head and face
- some were four-footed, others two-footed
- had interesting ornamentation on their head

THYREOPHORANS
(The name means "shield bearers.")
- ate plants
- walked on four legs
- had bony plates and spikes protecting their body
- two types: ankylosaurians (heavily armored back) and stegosaurs (plates and spikes on back and tail)

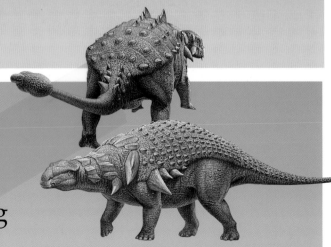

Top to bottom: *Euoplocephalus*, an ankylosaur, and *Edmontonia*, a nodosaur.

Geological Time Chart
What Happened When

ERA	PERIOD	YEARS AGO*	AGE	IMPORTANT EVENTS
CENOZOIC	**Quaternary:** Holocene Epoch	10,000 years ago to present	Age of MAMMALS	Cities appear (about 5,000 years ago).
	Pleistocene Epoch	1.65 mya to 10,000 years ago		Anatomically modern humans appear (about 200,000 years ago); cave painters (about 50,000 years ago).
	Tertiary: Pliocene Epoch	5 to 1.65 mya		Human ancestors (*Australopithecus*) appear (about 4 mya).
	Miocene Epoch	23 to 5 mya		Grazing mammals become more widespread.
	Oligocene Epoch	35 to 23 mya		Many mammals start evolving into modern forms.
	Eocene Epoch	57 to 35 mya		The Himalaya Mountains start to rise when India crashes into Asia (about 45 mya).
	Paleocene Epoch	65 to 57 mya		Many new kinds of mammals evolve.
MESOZOIC	Cretaceous	145 to 65 mya	Age of REPTILES	Dinosaurs dominate the land; many new, exotic forms. First flowering plants. At the end of this period, dinosaurs (except birds), pterosaurs, most marine reptiles, and many other animals and plants become extinct.
	Jurassic	208 to 145 mya		Pliosaurs appear. Dinosaurs dominate the land; mammals remain small. Appearance of first birds.
	Triassic	245 to 208 mya		The first dinosaurs appear; so do frogs, turtles, crocodilians, pterosaurs, and the first mammals. Plesiosaurs appear.

Era	Period	Time	Age	Description
	Permian	290 to 245 mya		Reptiles become the most common large animals on land. Time of the sailfin reptiles. This period ends with the greatest extinction event in Earth's history.
PALEOZOIC	Carboniferous	362 to 290 mya	Age of AMPHIBIANS	Time of great forests. (Over millions of years, their remains become coal.) The first winged insects appear. Late in this period, the first reptiles evolve.
	Devonian	408 to 362 mya	Age of FISHES	Sharks appear; so do armored fish. The first forests evolve; trees grow up to 30 feet tall. Near the end of this period, the first seed-producing plants appear, and the first amphibians evolve from fish.
	Silurian	440 to 408 mya		Plants begin to grow on land. The first jawed fish appear. There are fish in fresh-water as well as in oceans. Millipedes and scorpions move on to land.
	Ordovician	510 to 440 mya		First coral reefs appear. There also are nautiloids (NAW-till-oydz), squidlike creatures with long, pointy or coiled shells.
	Cambrian	570 to 510 mya		Many kinds of creatures appear in the oceans, including sponges. Also, the first shelled animals—clamlike brachiopods (BRAK-ee-oh-podz), and trilobites (TRY-loh-bites) that crawl over the sea floor. Fish appear—the first creatures with a backbone.
Precambrian		4.5 bya to 570 mya		Earth forms (around 4.5 bya). Life on Earth begins (around 3.8 bya).

*bya = billions of years ago ● mya = millions of years ago

Dinosaur Times

Dinosaurs have lived on Earth for over 230 million years—much longer than humans have. But not all dinosaur species (kinds) lived at the same time. Many different species came and went during those years.

Allosaurus

Allosaurus (AL-uh-SORE-us) and *Tyrannosaurus* (ty-RAN-uh-SORE-us) were both massive meat-eaters. But *Allosaurus* lived about as many years before *Tyrannosaurus* as *Tyrannosaurus* lived before us humans. A *Tyrannosaurus* may even have stubbed its toe on 70-million-year-old fossilized *Allosaurus* bones sticking out of the ground!

Tyrannosaurus

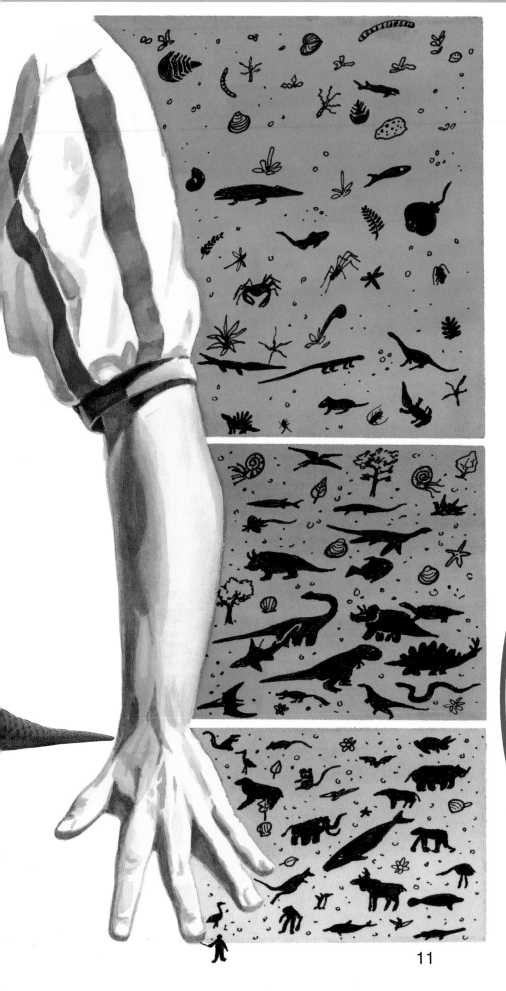

How much longer were dinosaurs on Earth than humans? If you look at your arm and imagine that the very first life on Earth happened at your shoulder, dinosaurs began near your elbow and lived on Earth to your wrist. Humans have been here only for the bit of time represented by the tip of one of your fingernails!

DID YOU KNOW....?
Dinosaurs have lived all over the planet. Dinosaur fossils have been found on every continent—including Antarctica. Dinosaurs lived in swamps, forests, and very dry areas.

Before the Dinosaurs

Fossil of a Precambrian jellyfish

Dinosaurs were not the first animals on Earth. Animals living in the Precambrian had very few hard parts, such as bones or shells, that would make good fossils. Only a few places on Earth show a record of life from this early time.

In a fossil-rich area of Canada called the Burgess Shale, rocks are as much as 530 million years old! Among the fossils in these rocks are some really weird-looking Cambrian animals. One is a 25-inch-long beast with two eyes on stalks. Another is a five-eyed wormlike animal.

Some trilobites (TRY-loh-bites) survived until the end of the Permian Period, but they were at their peak in the Ordovician. Up to 27 inches long, the trilobite's name comes from the fact that its body is divided length-wise into three parts. (*Tri* means "three"; *lobe* means "part.") Trilobites are the earliest fossil animals to show well-developed eyes.

A trilobite crawls at the bottom center of this Ordovician sea scene.

Sea-scorpions, or eurypterids (yur-IPP-tur-idz), scuttled across muddy Silurian waters. Some grew to longer than five feet! Some scorpions had moved onto land earlier— they probably were distant relatives of the eurypterids.

Eurypterid fossils

Ichthyostega

Ichthyostega (ICK-thee-oh-STEG-uh), from the Late Devonian Period, may have been one of the first four-legged animals to walk on land. It was an amphibian—an animal that can live on land but must lay its eggs in water so they don't dry out. *Ichthyostega* probably spent a lot of time hunting in the water.

Dunkleosteus

Ammonite

There were some new hunters in Carboniferous seas. Ammonites (AM-uh-nites) looked a bit like squid stuffed into big snail shells. They ate trilobites and other shellfish.

Dunkleosteus (left) was one of the largest ocean predators of the Late Devonian Period. It grew close to 20 feet long! It was heavily armored with bony plates that shielded its head, sides, and upper back. Its sharp dental plates worked like teeth to grind up its prey.

DID YOU KNOW. . . ?
Reptiles first appeared in the Late Carboniferous Period. Their eggs had a protective shell, so reptiles could do something that amphibians could not: lay their eggs on land.

At the end of the Carboniferous Period, there were some very big insects around. One, very much like a dragonfly, had a wingspan of up to 2.5 feet. There was also a centipedelike creature that grew up to 6.5 feet long, and a spider about 14 inches wide!

Moschops

The plant-eating *Moschops* (MAHS-kops) may look pretty tame, but don't let that fool you. *Moschops* had powerful legs and very thick skull bones on the top of its head. This reptile of the Permian Period possibly used its thick skull to head-butt other *Moschops*, the way some modern-day goats do.

Two sailfin reptiles: carnivore *Dimetrodon* (upper left) and herbivore *Edaphosaurus* (lower right).

Imagine a seashore with 10-foot-long, fin-backed reptiles soaking up the sun! *Dimetrodon* (dye-MEET-row-don), a meat-eater, and plant-eating *Edaphosaurus* (ee-DAF-uh-SORE-us) had fins supported by long spines growing from their back-bone. These reptiles died out millions of years before the first dinosaurs appeared.

Mesosaurus

Mesosaurus (left), one of the oldest known aquatic (water-dwelling) reptiles, lived in the shallow, coastal waters of South America and Africa during the Permian Period. About three feet long, it had teeth, but used them to sift food from the water, not to chew.

Some of the animals found in Permian seas.

This fossil of an animal that lived during the Late Permian was found in Texas.

DID YOU KNOW. . . ?
The end of the Permian Period was marked by one of the biggest extinction events in Earth's history! As much as 90 percent of life may have been wiped out. This may have helped clear the way for the rise of the dinosaurs.

Life in the Triassic

By the end of the Permian Period, the continents had bunched together (see map, far right) into a supercontinent called Pangaea (pan-JEE-uh). But by the end of the Triassic, Pangaea was breaking up —very slowly. All over the world, the climate was warmer than it is today—there was less difference in temperature between the poles and the equator.

Some plants from this scene of 220 million years ago still exist, including conifers, ginkgoes, ferns, and palm-like cycads.

Left to right: *Plateosaurus*, *Coelophysis*, and *Lystrosaurus*.

Earth during the Triassic Period — Pangaea (Europe & Asia, North America, South America, Africa, India, Antarctica, Australia)

Erythrosuchus (uh-RITH-rah-soo-kus) and *Euparkeria* (yoo-par-KEE-ree-uh) were meat-eating reptiles of the Early Triassic. They weren't dinosaurs, but probably were closely related to the ancestors of the dinosaur. In its day, *Erythrosuchus* was one of the biggest predators on land. You can see why some plant-eaters from this time had body armor!

Erythrosuchus

Euparkeria

Plateosaurus (PLAT-ee-uh-sore-us) is a commonly found Late Triassic fossil. One of the first large dinosaurs, it grew to 26 feet long. ● **Coelophysis** (SEEL-uh-FYE-sis) may be the best-known of the oldest dinosaurs, because so many of its fossilized remains have been found. It arose in the Late Triassic. Its size ranged from just over three feet to ten feet in length. ● **Lystrosaurus** (LIS-trah-sore-us) was not a dinosaur. It was a plant-eater that might have used its small tusks to defend itself against meat-eaters. It was a little over three feet long.

19

Triassic Plant-eaters

The first plant-eating dinosaurs appeared during the Triassic. Some of them belonged to a group known as prosauropods (proh-SORE-uh-podz), because they look a little like sauropods, a later dinosaur group that included *Apatosaurus* (uh-PAT-uh-SORE-us). Scientists think that these groups had a common ancestor.

The biggest and heaviest prosauropod discovered so far is the 40-foot-long *Melanosaurus* (muh-LAN-oh-SORE-us), found in South Africa.

An adult *Mussaurus*

The tiny skeleton of a baby *Mussaurus* (muh-SORE-us) is one of the smallest dinosaur skeletons (except for those still in eggs) yet found. Its skull is just over an inch long and the entire skeleton fits into a man's cupped hands. *Mussaurus*, found in present-day Argentina, was a prosauropod that lived about 215 million years ago. Its name means "mouse lizard."

We have only a few bones from the prosauropod *Agrosaurus* (AG-roh-SORE-us). In 1844, an explorer from a British ship went ashore in Australia and did some digging around. He found *Agrosaurus* bones—the first Australian dinosaur fossils found and the only ones from the Triassic Period.

A *Plateosaurus* herd caught in a flash flood

Did *Plateosaurus* travel in herds? The remains of many *Plateosaurus* were found in one spot. That could mean that something killed a herd all at once—or that bones from different times and places were swept into one place by heavy rains.

WORDS FOR THE WISE

The name of this group of dinosaurs—prosauropods—describes them quite well! *Pro* means "earlier than," *sauros* means "lizard," and *pod* means "foot."

Little *Pisanosaurus* hides from a larger meat-eater.

Pisanosaurus (pye-SAN-uh-SORE-us) might be the oldest known member of the ornithischian (bird-hipped) dinosaur group. It lived about 225 million years ago, in what is now Argentina. Scientists guess that it was probably a fast, two-legged runner.

22

Triassic Meat-eaters

The first dinosaurs evolved from meat-eating reptiles. Some of the earliest dinosaurs we know of—from as long as 225 million years ago—were also meat-eaters. Lizard-hipped, meat-eating dinosaurs are called theropods (THAIR-uh-podz).

Three-foot-long *Eoraptor* (EE-oh-RAP-tur), a very early dinosaur found in present-day Argentina, had many features that differed from later dinosaurs. Even its teeth were unusual: Some look like a carnivore's, while others look more like a plant-eater's.

At one time, nine-foot-long *Coelophysis* was thought to be a cannibal (ate its own kind). Scientists had found hundreds of *Coelophysis* skeletons at a site in New Mexico, and some, like this one, had small bones inside.

However, in mid 2006, it was discovered that the bones were that of a relative of the crocodile.

Staurikosaurus

Staurikosaurus (STAW-ri-kuh-SORE-us) is one of the earliest dinosaurs known. This slim, seven-foot-long dinosaur ran on two legs. *Staurikosaurus* skeletons have been found in South America. Their sharp teeth and claws tell us that they ate meat.

The name *Saltopus* (SAWL-toh-pus) means "leaping foot," but this animal used its long hind legs to run, not leap. About the size of a cat, *Saltopus* was fast, which helped it catch and devour prey. So did its long neck, clawed fingers, and sharp teeth. Was *Saltopus* a dinosaur? For a while, experts said yes; now, most say no, but it is a close relative.

Syntarsus (sin-TAR-sus) was a Late Triassic theropod. It got its name, which means "fused ankle," because some of its ankle bones had grown together. Only two feet tall, *Syntarsus* had to avoid being eaten by larger theropods while it searched for smaller prey.

Pterosaurs

Rhamphorhynchus

The first pterosaurs (TER-uh-sores) appeared in the Triassic. The last ones vanished at the end of the Cretaceous. Pterosaurs are not dinosaurs, but they took to the skies during dinosaur times.

There were two kinds of pterosaurs. Those like *Rhamphorhynchus* (RAM-fohr-ING-kus) were quite small and had long tails. The other group included *Pterodactylus* (TARE-oh-DAK-til-us) and had longer necks and shorter tails than the first group.

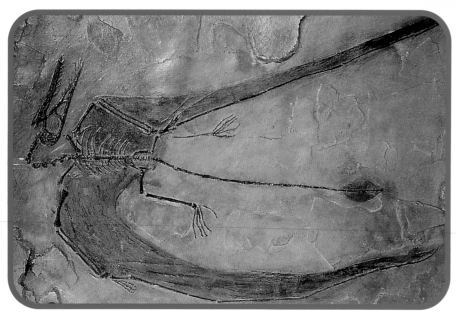

Fossil of a Jurassic *Rhamphorhynchus*

Rhamphorhynchus ate fish. We know this because some *Rhamphorhynchus* fossils have fish bones in their stomachs. This reptile was 18 inches long, with a short neck, a long tail, and a wide wingspan. Its long, pointed jaws were filled with sharp teeth that angled outward. *Rhamphorhynchus* probably flew over the water, snatching up fish near the surface.

Quetzalcoatlus (KET-sol-koh-AT-lus) was one of the biggest flying creatures of all time. It cruised over Late Cretaceous Texas on thin wings that may have stretched nearly 40 feet wide (wider than a modern biplane's). Some scientists think that it may have lived much as modern vultures do.

The body of a *Pteranodon* (terr-AN-oh-dahn) was only about the size of a turkey's, but its head—counting the long crest—was 6 feet long! It had a huge wingspan, too: nearly 30 feet wide.

Pteranodon

Life in the Jurassic

Jurassic
sea scene

During the Jurassic Period, Pangaea continued to break up (see map, far right). The Atlantic Ocean began to form as Africa and the Americas split apart. India started its drift toward Asia. Jurassic skies were populated by flying reptiles (*see pp. 30-31*), the seas by marine reptiles. Dinosaurs dominated the land.

Plesiosaurs (PLEE-zee-oh-sores) were not dinosaurs. These Mesozoic creatures, which grew from 8 to 40 feet long, were among the largest marine reptiles. They used their powerful paddle-limbs to "fly" through the water after fish and squid, much as sea turtles do today.

Fossil of a Jurassic Period shrimp

Plesiosaurus

Ichthyosaurs were marine reptiles that appeared during the Triassic and lived through the Jurassic and into the Cretaceous. The ichthyosaur *Ophthalmosaurus* (ahf-THAL-muh-SORE-us), below, had large eyes. (*Ophthalmo-* means "eye" or "eyeball.") These may have helped it hunt for food in the darkness of deep waters.

Ophthalmosaurus

Jurassic
land
scene

During the Jurassic, conifers (trees in the same family as today's redwoods and pines), palmlike cycads (SYE-kadz), and ginkgo trees grew in forests. Dinosaurs were among the largest, but small mammals and other creatures also roamed the land.

Plant-eating dinosaurs and meat-eating dinosaurs shared the same land areas. Large meat-eaters hunted smaller prey, some of which traveled in groups for protection. Above, a lone meat-eating *Dilophosaurus* (die-LOH-fuh-SORE-us) has its eye on a herd of plant-eating *Anchisaurus* (ANG-kee-SORE-us).

At left: A meat-eating dinosaur is attacking a terrified *Heterodontosaurus* (HET-ur-uh-DON-toh-SORE-us), which may have eaten plants or animals or both.

Jurassic Plant-eaters

Jurassic plant-eaters included some of the biggest animals ever to walk on Earth. Some were three times as tall as a giraffe and as long as one-and-a-half blue whales! Lizard-hipped, plant-eating dinosaurs with a long neck and tail are called sauropods (SORE-uh-podz).

Seismosaurus from the side, front, and back.

No one has found a complete *Seismosaurus* (SIZE-muh-SORE-us) yet. Based on bones found so far, though, scientists think that it was 130 to 170 feet long. (That's about half the length of a football field!) Most of its length was in its neck and tail. Like other sauropods, *Seismosaurus* seems to have swallowed stones to help grind up food in its stomach.

Brachiosaurus (BRAK-ee-uh-SORE-us) may have weighed as much as 12 elephants, and was more than 70 feet long and 40 feet high. (It would have had no problem peeking over the top of a four-story building!) Its bones have been found in western North America and in East Africa.

Seismosaurus from above.

Diplodocus (dih-PLOH-duh-kus) had a very small head. How small? Imagine that your body stays the same size, but your head shrinks to the size of a peanut! How could an animal with such a little head and pencil-like teeth eat enough to keep its huge body alive? We don't know, but it must have managed quite well: Sauropods thrived on Earth for more than 140 million years!

Diplodocus

Paleontologists were surprised by what they found when they studied the remains of *Shunosaurus* (SHOO-nuh-SORE-us). The bones at the end of its long tail bulge out to form a club—with spines on it!

Shunosaurus

Mamenchisaurus (mah-MEN-chih-SORE-us) was 70 feet long—and half of that was its neck! That puts it in the record books as having the longest neck of any animal ever known. Its name comes from where it was found: Mamenchi, China.

Besides the great sauropods, other plant-eating dinosaurs grazed their way through the Jurassic.

Toothed dinosaurs had only one kind of teeth: either the kind that grinds up plants or the kind that tears into flesh. *Heterodontosaurus* had three kinds (as do humans): sharp teeth in the front, longer teeth (fangs) on each side, and wider teeth in back. It was among the first dinosaurs to have cheeks—a place to hold food while chewing.

Heterodontosaurus head (above) and skull (below).

Camptosaurus

Several different species of *Camptosaurus* (KAMP-tuh-SORE-us) lived in North America and Europe near the end of the Jurassic. This 20-foot-long ornithischian (bird-hipped dinosaur) probably walked on its hind legs most of the time, but sometimes walked on all four.

Anchisaurus

Some prosauropods—the earliest-known plant-eating dinosaurs—were still around during the Jurassic Period. Some were large, like 30-foot-long *Riojasaurus* (ree-OH-hah-SORE-us). Others, such as *Anchisaurus* (ANG-kee-SORE-us), never reached 10 feet.

Riojasaurus

Jurassic Stegosaurs

Stegosaurs (STEG-uh-sores) were dinosaurs whose bodies had an armor made of plates, spikes, or both. Clearly, these Jurassic plant-eaters did *not* want to become a meat-eater's next meal!

The rows of plates along the back of 25-foot-long *Stegosaurus* (STEG-uh-SORE-us) may have helped the animal control its body temperature by soaking up the sun to warm its body, or by releasing heat to cool it. *Stegosaurus* had four heavy spikes, nearly four feet long, at the end of its tail.

Left: A herd of armor-plated *Scutellosaurus* fleeing from a *Dilophosaurus*.

More than 300 armor plates were found with the skeleton of a *Scutellosaurus* (skoo-TELL-uh-SORE-us). The living animal may have had more.

DID YOU KNOW. . . ?
Even the biggest stegosaurs had brains that were no larger than a dog's.

Kentrosaurus

Kentrosaurus (KEN-truh-SORE-us) had plates about half-way down its back. From there to the tip of its tail, this 15-foot-long plant-eater had pairs of spikes! It also had a pair of spikes coming out from its shoulders. The spikes probably served *Kentrosaurus* as a defense against predators.

Jurassic Meat-eaters

Jurassic theropods (meat-eating dinosaurs that walked on their hind legs) came in both large and small sizes.

Dilophosaurus on the prowl

With twin crests decorating the top of its head, *Dilophosaurus* (dye-LOH-fuh-SORE-us) certainly stood out. About 20 feet long, it had long, slender teeth and a lightly built skull. This makes scientists think that it may have been more of a scavenger than an active hunter. (A scavenger eats already-dead or injured animals.)

Dilophosaurus skull

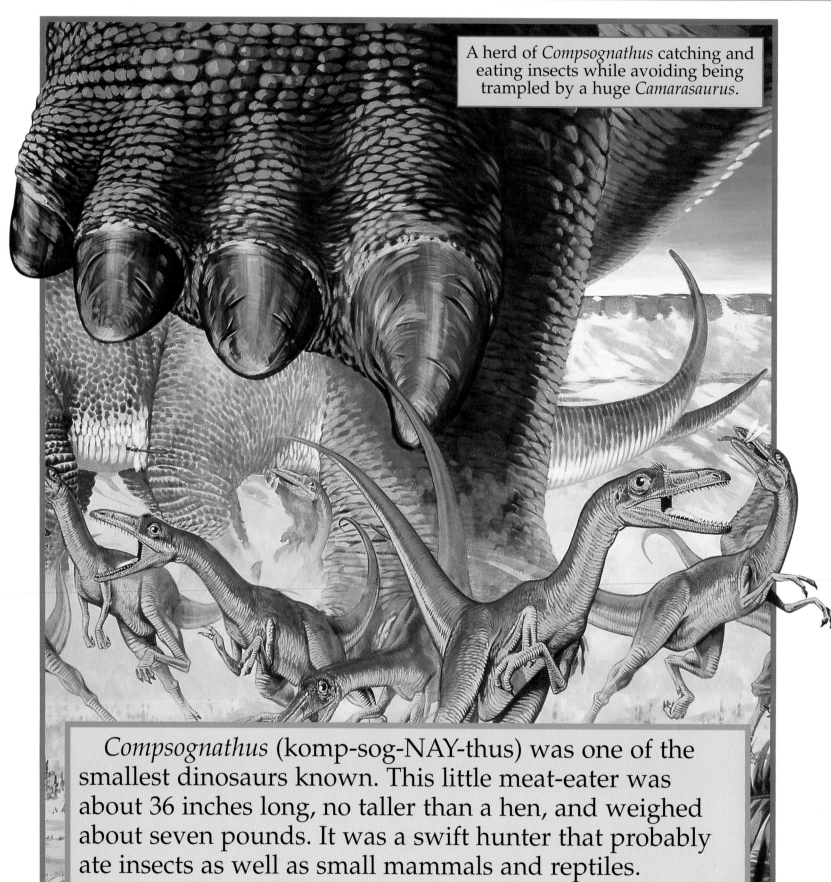

A herd of *Compsognathus* catching and eating insects while avoiding being trampled by a huge *Camarasaurus*.

Compsognathus (komp-sog-NAY-thus) was one of the smallest dinosaurs known. This little meat-eater was about 36 inches long, no taller than a hen, and weighed about seven pounds. It was a swift hunter that probably ate insects as well as small mammals and reptiles.

Megalosaurus (MEG-uh-luh-SORE-us) was the first non-avian dinosaur to be named. Its name, which means "big lizard," really fits: *Megalosaurus* was 30 feet long and, when standing, 12 feet tall! Like all theropods, its long tail probably helped it keep its balance.

Allosaurus attacking a young *Diplodocus*.

With its light skeleton and long legs, *Ornitholestes* (OR-nih-thuh-LES-teez) must have been a very quick runner. The name *Ornitholestes* means "bird robber," but it probably ate small reptiles, mammals, and frogs—and other dinosaurs.

Allosaurus (AL-uh-SORE-us), which was 30 to 40 feet long, had big, strong hind legs that may have allowed it to run almost 20 miles an hour. Its head, alone, was as big as an entire *Compsognathus*! Its jaws were packed with more than 73 teeth, each tooth being an inch long.

A Rustle of Feathers

When did the first bird appear? Are birds descendants of the dinosaurs? Paleontologists look for clues in rocks from the Jurassic and Cretaceous periods. Fossils of flying animals are rare. Most flew over land, so when they died, their bodies were probably eaten by other animals before they could be preserved. Their light bones, which helped them fly, would have broken easily.

Sinosauropteryx

Caudipteryx

Caudipteryx (kaw-DIP-ter-iks), a feathered dinosaur, seems to be on the border between non-avian (not a bird) dinosaurs and birds. About three feet long, it was a swift runner that didn't have the right bone structure to fly.

Sinosauropteryx (SYE-noh-sore-OP-ter-iks), found in China, was a chicken-sized, meat-eating dinosaur. It is clearly not a bird, but its fossils have something different from those of most other fossil dinosaurs: things that look like feathers! It was closely related to the ancestor of today's birds.

42

This fossil, found in Germany, is one of the most famous in the world. It is *Archaeopteryx* (AR-kee-OP-ter-iks), which lived 150 million years ago. This small, meat-eating dinosaur is the earliest-known feathered animal. The shape of its feathers suggests that it did more than just glide—it actually flew, but probably not far.

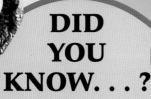

DID YOU KNOW. . . ?
Most experts say that dinosaurs are not extinct! They remain on Earth—in the form of their descendants, birds.

Some well-preserved fossils were found in China recently. Several are of an early bird called *Confuciusornis* (kon-FYOO-shuh-SORE-nis). Unlike *Archaeopteryx*, which had a mouth full of teeth, *Confuciusornis* had a toothless beak similar to that of modern birds. It is the earliest-known bird that was able to fly for any distance.

Top: *Confuciusornis*, 120 million years old. Bottom: Old World oriole, a modern-day bird.

Life in the Cretaceous

It was a wet world during the Cretaceous Period. The seas rose more than 600 feet higher than today's level. That covered almost half of what is now dry land. In North America, an inland sea grew and shrank several times. Mountains rose and volcanoes erupted along the west coast of the Americas. The climate was warmer then: There was no ice to be found—not even at the poles!

This painting shows some of the dinosaurs that lived during the Cretaceous— at various times and in various parts of the world.

The marine lizard above, *Tylosaurus* (TY-loh-SORE-us), was not a dinosaur. It swam in the sea that stretched across North America, from the Arctic Ocean to the Gulf of Mexico, during the Late Cretaceous. *Tylosaurus* grew up to 45 feet long. Its limbs were flippers rather than arms and legs. It used its gigantic jaws and sharp teeth to snap up fish and other sea animals.

Earth during the Cretaceous Period

DID YOU KNOW. . . ? The first flowering plants appeared during the Cretaceous Period. This made a big change in how the world looked!

Duckbills

One group of Cretaceous plant-eating dinosaurs was called hadrosaurs (HAD-ruh-sores). They had long, wide snouts ending in broad beaks that looked something like a duck's bill. From that came their nickname: the duckbilled dinosaurs.

Duckbills' teeth were crammed into their jaws in stacks of three to five replacement teeth under each working tooth. Up to 60 stacks and 1,200 teeth were packed into a single duckbill mouth!

A duckbill skull

From a distant shore, a hunting *Tyrannosaurus* eyes herds of various kinds of duckbilled dinosaurs.

There were two kinds of duckbills. Those like *Anatosaurus* (ah-NAT-uh-SORE-us), at right, had a flat head without a bony crest. The other group, which included *Lambeosaurus* (LAM-bee-uh-SORE-us), below, had fancy, hollow crests.

Shantungosaurus (SHAN-tung-uh-SORE-us), above, lived in China. The biggest of all duckbills, it was about 50 feet long and weighed around nine tons.

The name *Maiasaura* (MY-uh-SORE-uh) means "good mother lizard." Paleontologist John Horner named this duckbilled dinosaur after he found fossils, in Montana in 1979, suggesting that it took care of its babies. Until *Maiasaura* was found, scientists thought that dinosaurs just laid their eggs and left the babies to take care of themselves after they hatched, as most reptiles do.

Each *Maiasaura* mother shaped her seven-foot-wide nest out of dirt and laid her eggs. Then she covered them with plants and dirt, to help keep them warm. Maiasaur parents apparently took food back to the nest for their young. Adults probably spit up food that they had already chewed and partially digested. This would be easier for the babies to eat.

Iguanodon

Iguanodon (ih-GWAHN-uh-don) was a plant-eating dinosaur of the Early Cretaceous. It was only the second dinosaur ever described. British amateur paleontologist Gideon Mantell studied fossil teeth found in a gravel pit. He guessed right when he said that they were for chewing plants. Since the teeth looked like an iguana's, he decided that they must have come from a huge, iguanalike animal.

Iguanodon under attack by small theropods.

DID YOU KNOW . . . ?

Iguanodon had no front teeth, but its back teeth were wide and flat. Today's herbivores use teeth like that for grinding the plants they eat. At the front of *Iguanodon*'s jaws was a horny, self-sharpening beak much like that of a tortoise. This worked well for chomping twigs and leaves.

Iguanodon was about 30 feet long, with a long, heavy tail that probably helped it keep its balance—whether it walked on its back legs, as young ones did, or on all fours, as larger, heavier ones did. *Iguanodon* tracks have been found in rocks throughout Europe.

Iguanodon's bony thumbs

Early drawings of *Iguanodon* show it with a spiky horn on its nose. That "horn" was really a pointed, bony thumb (above). But no one realized that until a skeleton was found with the bone in the right place.

In 1878, 24 nearly complete *Iguanodon* skeletons were found in a Belgian coal mine. The skeletons helped give scientists a much better idea of what *Iguanodon* looked like.

More Cretaceous Plant-eaters

Ten-foot-long *Dravidosaurus* (druh-VID-uh-SORE-us) is one of the only stegosaurs known from near the end of dinosaur times.

Cretaceous herbivores (plant-eaters) came in assorted sizes.

Hypsilopho-don (HIP-suh-LOH-fuh-don), below, was only about seven-and-a-half feet long. Walking with its tail up and head forward, it would have been about two feet off the ground at its hips.

Alamosaurus (AL-uh-moh-SORE-us)— one of the biggest Cretaceous plant-eaters—was nearly 70 feet long.

Ouranosaurus (oo-RAN-oh-SORE-us) was about 24 feet long and had long projections on its backbone. It may have had a sail like *Spinosaurus* (SPY-nuh-SORE-us), a meat-eating dinosaur that lived in about the same time and place.

Stegoceras (steg-OH-ser-us) was one of the dinosaurs nicknamed "bone-heads." Its dome-shaped skull had a roof of bone three inches thick, with a spiky frill. What was it for? Experts used to think that *Stegoceras* males butted heads, as bighorn sheep do today, but no one really knows.

Above: An *Alamosaurus* trio defends itself from an *Albertosaurus* attack.

53

Plant-eaters in Armor

Some Cretaceous plant-eaters relied on armor to keep them from becoming another dinosaur's lunch. Armored dinosaurs belong to a family called Ankylosauria (an-KYE-low-SORE-ee-ah). That name means "fused lizards."

Edmontonia (ED-mon-TOH-nee-uh) was the largest of the nodosaurs. It grew to a length of about 25 feet. Predators had to beware of those spikes coming from its sides!

Ankylosaurs and nodosaurs (NOH-doh-sores) were two types of dinosaurs in the Ankylosauria group. Both had bony plates called osteoderms protecting their bodies. Ankylosaurs had wide heads, and clubs at the end of their tails. Nodosaurs had narrow heads, sideways-pointing spikes, and tails without clubs.

The smallest known member of Ankylosauria was *Struthiosaurus* (STROO-thee-oh-SORE-us), a six-foot-long nodosaur.

54

Minmi (MIN-my) was a nodosaur. A blanket of very small osteoderms protected its tender stomach. *Minmi* was named for a rock formation in Australia, where it was found.

Euoplocephalus (yoo-OP-luh-SEF-uh-lus) was an ankylosaur—look at that tail! It had spikes, and was armored from head to tail. It even had armored eyelids that could be shut like window shades to protect its eyes.

55

Plant-eaters with Horns

One group of Cretaceous plant-eating dinosaurs is called ceratopsians (SER-uh-TOP-see-uns). That means "horned faces"—and you can see why! These rhinoceroslike animals had a wide assortment of bony horns and neck frills.

Right: *Styracosaurus* (sty-RAK-uh-SORE-us), seemed to have horns and spikes sticking out all over its head. The spikes on its frill probably were used for display.

Triceratops (try-SER-uh-tops) was 25 feet long and weighed more than an elephant. Its skull alone was over six feet long!

56

Torosaurus had a huge head. One skeleton was found with a head 8.5 feet long—the second-biggest head of any land animal ever known! The frill of a *Torosaurus* was even longer than its head.

Left: This *Triceratops* herd is circling to protect its young while using its horns to defend itself from a *Tyrannosaurus* attack.

Not all ceratopsians were large. *Microceratops* (MYE-kroh-SER-uh-tops) was one of the smallest of all dinosaurs: only 30 inches long! The group of *Microceratops* below is hiding from a *Tarbosaurus*.

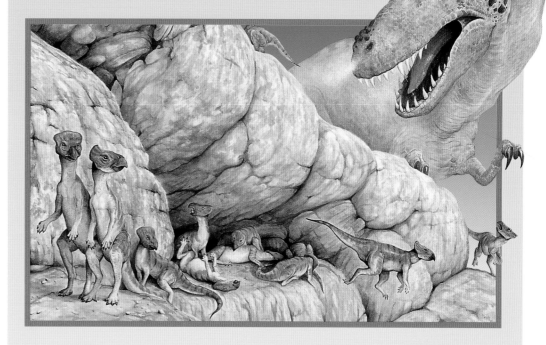

57

Cretaceous Hunters

Cretaceous meat-eating dinosaurs came in all shapes and sizes.

A *Baryonyx* claw fossil

Talons nearly one foot long earned *Baryonyx* (BAYR-ee-ON-iks) the nickname "Claws." This 30-foot-long, Early Cretaceous dinosaur was expert at catching fish, its favorite food. It had a long snout filled with teeth, something like a crocodile's. *Baryonyx* had twice as many teeth as other toothed meat-eating dinosaurs!

58

One of the largest meat-eaters ever, 40-foot-long *Spinosaurus* (SPINE-uh-SORE-us) had projections up to 6.5 feet long coming out of its backbone. What was that "sail" for? The extra skin surface may have helped *Spinosaurus* get more heat from the sun when it was cold, and cool down its huge body when it was hot.

Acrocanthosaurus (AK-roh-KAN-thuh-SORE-us) had foot-long projections on the bones of its neck, back, and tail. Unlike *Spinosaurus*'s thin sail, these projections were covered in a thick ridge of flesh. Strong muscles attached to the projections gave *Acrocanthosaurus* great power for catching and tearing apart prey.

Dromaeosaurus (DROH-mee-uh-SORE-us) had a large brain and big eyes in its birdlike head. Just six feet long, it was probably a smart, quick hunter that grabbed small prey, then ripped into it with a special toe claw.

Below: Little *Dromaeosaurus* feeding on prey killed by a larger hunter.

Utahraptor (YOO-tah-RAP-tor), at right, was a larger relative of *Dromaeosaurus*. It has been called one of the most intelligent—and vicious—of all non-avian dinosaurs. Its toe claw may have been more than 15 inches long.

Utahraptor

A movie-model version of *Velociraptor*

Velociraptor is a well-named dinosaur. This child-sized hunter's name means "swift thief," and it was built for speed, with a light-boned body and long, sturdy legs. It was also built for catching and killing prey: Its hands and feet ended in big, sharp claws.

Oviraptor (OH-vee-RAP-tor) means "egg thief," because the first *Oviraptor* fossil found (in the 1920s) was on top of eggs thought to belong to *Protoceratops*. But in 1993, an oviraptorid embryo was found inside an egg of the same type! The fossil above is of a mother oviraptorid with her own eggs.

61

Ostrich-mimics

A group of ostrichlike dinosaurs lived during the Late Cretaceous. They ran swiftly on long, thin hind legs. They probably ate small reptiles, mammals, and insects. Scientists think that they may also have eaten the eggs of other animals.

WORDS FOR THE WISE

The scientific name for this group of dinosaurs is ornithomimids (OR-nith-oh-MYE-midz). It comes from two Greek words that perfectly describe what they are: *ornith*, meaning "bird," and *mimos*, meaning "imitator"!

At left: *Gallimimus* (GAL-ih-MYE-mus), 26 feet long, was the biggest ostrich-mimic dinosaur.

Dromiceiomimus

Twelve-foot-long *Dromiceio-mimus* (DROH-mee-see-uh-MYE-mus) may have been one of the fastest non-avian dinosaurs. It may have been able to run up to 40 miles an hour! It could use that speed in two ways: to catch up to prey, and to escape from larger predators.

Below: *Struthiomimus*

Struthiomimus (STROO-thee-uh-MYE-mus) was 10 to 13 feet long and 8 feet tall. Its long, strong hands ended in three claw-tipped fingers. It probably wasn't the fastest ornithomimid, but even at half speed it could have kept pace with a world-class human athlete in a 100-meter race!

Troodon

Troodon (TROH-oh-don)—a human-sized, meat-eating dinosaur—had a lot of brain for its body size. It was one of the smartest of all non-avian dinosaurs.

Troodon skull

Troodon's sharp teeth, long claws, and other features mark it as a swift-running hunter and meat-eater.

With its long, slim tail to help balance its long, thin legs, *Troodon* was probably very speedy—and good at making quick turns. The long fingers on its hands would have been good for snatching up small reptiles and mammals.

Each of *Troodon*'s eyes was almost two inches wide. Such big eyes may mean that it hunted in low light, at dusk or nighttime.

Troodon had many sharp teeth, hence its name: *troo* is Greek for "to wound"; *don*, for "tooth."

Deinonychus

Scientists used to think that meat-eating non-avian dinosaurs were slow-moving animals. But in 1964, *Deinonychus* (dye-NON-ih-kus) was discovered—and made scientists rethink their ideas.

Deinonychus had long, strong arms ending in three-fingered hands with sharp claws. It could grab and hold on to prey.

On the second toe of each foot, *Deinonychus* had a curved claw that was up to five inches long. The dinosaur may have balanced on one foot and kicked at prey with the other, using the claw to make deep wounds. The claws stayed sharp because they were held off the ground when *Deinonychus* walked or ran.

Hunting alone, *Deinonychus* probably ate small reptiles and mammals. There is some evidence that it hunted in packs; if two or three teamed up, they could have handled larger prey with ease.

DID YOU KNOW. . . ?
The name *Deinonychus* means "terrible claw."

Deinonychus was 10 feet long, but light for its size. (It probably weighed about the same as an adult human.) Its tail, stiffened by bony tendons, stuck nearly straight out. This helped *Deinonychus* balance as it jumped and ran.

67

Tyrannosaurus & Company

Tyrannosaurus (tye-RAN-uh-SORE-us) may be the most famous dinosaur of all. At 40 to 50 feet long, this giant was one of the biggest meat-eaters to ever walk on Earth.

Was *Tyrannosaurus* an active hunter or did it just look for dead animals to eat? Like many of today's meat-eaters, it probably did both.

68

Old models of *Tyrannosaurus* show it standing up with its tail on the ground. Today, we know that it leaned forward with its tail up and out, to balance its large, heavy head.

The head of a *Tyrannosaurus* was more than 4.5 feet long!

DID YOU KNOW....?

Tyrannosaurus belongs to a group of dinosaurs, called tyrannosaurids (tye-RAN-uh-SAW-ridz), that looked a lot like it.

(Turn the page to see some of its relatives.)

Tyrannosaurus teeth (below left, and at right) were one inch wide and up to six inches long. They were shaped and serrated like steak knives, to cut through flesh and bone. Scientists think that *Tyrannosaurus* could rip off a 500-pound chunk of meat with just one bite of its powerful jaws!

69

There is no doubt that *Carcharodontosaurus* (kar-KAR-oh-DON-tuh-SORE-us) was a mighty meat-eater. Look at all these huge, sharp teeth! It is named for the great white shark (*Carcharodon megalodon*) whose teeth are similar.

DID YOU KNOW. . .? *Carcharodontosaurus* was only slightly bigger than *Tyrannosaurus rex*, which was around for only about the last 15 million years of dinosaur time.

70

At 26 feet in length, *Albertosaurus* (al-BUR-tuh-SORE-us) was big, but only about half the size of its huge relative, *Tyrannosaurus*. Though smaller, it was just as fierce a hunter. *Albertosaurus* lived at the end of the Cretaceous Period.

Two tyrannosaurids compete for food in this scene of life in the Late Cretaceous Period.

71

End of the Dinosaurs?

Most dinosaurs vanished at the end of the Cretaceous. Scientists are still trying to figure out why and how. No one idea seems to explain the whole story.

DON'T FORGET!
Most experts say that dinosaurs remain on Earth in the form of their descendants, birds.

One theory is that a bolide (a rock from space) crashed into Earth. This could have changed the environment, making it harmful to most dinosaurs. Some scientists think that the extinction occurred all at once. Others think that dinosaurs were already in trouble—the bolide just finished them off.

Dinosaurs were not the only type of life to face extinction around the end of the Cretaceous Period. Many other kinds of animals also disappeared then, too, including pterosaurs, and many marine animals. Many kinds of plants also died out.

The great seas were shrinking at the end of the Cretaceous. This may have let migrating dinosaurs mix with each other for the first time. Diseases or new predators may have killed off many dinosaurs. Older ideas about why most dinosaurs disappeared include new poisonous plants and mammals eating dinosaur eggs.

What Came Next

About 16 million years ago, the giant shark *Carcharodon megalodon* (kar-KAR-uh-don MEG-uh-la-don) began to hunt the seas. Scientists think that it was 40 to 45 feet long—about four times the length of today's fierce predator, the great white shark.

Teeth from a shark of 10 million years ago (left) and a great white shark of today.

With the majority of dinosaurs gone (birds remained), other kinds of animals moved into areas that dinosaurs had inhabited. Many different kinds of plants and animals evolved. Mammals—relatively minor in dinosaur days—became among the largest land animals on Earth.

The Cenozoic Era (mya = million years ago)

Paleocene Epoch 65 to 57 mya	Eocene Epoch 57 to 35 mya	Oligocene Epoch 35 to 25 mya	Miocene Epoch 23 to 5 mya	Pliocene Epoch 5 to 1.65 mya	Pleistocene Epoch 1.65 million to 10,000 years ago	Holocene Epoch 10,000 years ago to today

The first horse, *Hyracotherium* (HYE-rak-uh-THAIR-ee-um), was only about a foot tall. It evolved around the same time grasses did, but did not eat them—its teeth were not suited for grazing. Its descendants, however, became grazers.

Above: *Hyracotherium*

About two million years ago, a Great Ice Age began. Then, about 10,000 years ago, things began to warm up again. The climate changes were hard on animal life, and many species became extinct.

This painting shows a scene of plant and animal life in Europe during the Tertiary Period (65-1.65 mya). After the first grasses appeared, so did horses and other animals that lived by eating grass.

Photo Credits